Best Wishes

[signature]

TOBEY BOLAND

and the

BLACKSTONE CANAL

By

Thomas L. Rooney

Illustrated by

Patricia A. Foley-Donovan

Ambassador Books, Inc.
Worcester • Massachusetts

Library of Congress Cataloging-in-Publication Data

Rooney, Thomas L., 1929-
  Tobey Boland and the Blackstone Canal / by Thomas L. Rooney ; illustrated by Patricia A. Foley-Donovan.
    p. cm.
  ISBN 1-929039-30-1 (hardcover)
  1. Blackstone Canal (Mass.)--History--Juvenile literature. 2. Boland, Tobias, 1795-1888--Juvenile literature.
3. Civil engineers--Massachusetts--Biography--Juvenile literature. I. Foley-Donovan, Patricia A., ill. II. Title.

TC625.B6R66 2005
974.4'3--dc22
                              2005018855

Published in the United States by Ambassador Books, Inc.
91 Prescott Street, Worcester, Massachusetts 01605 • (800) 577-0909

Printed in China.

For current information about all titles from Ambassador Books, Inc.,
visit our website at: www.ambassadorbooks.com.

This book is dedicated to Vincent E. "Jake" Powers, Ph.D
who is a source of inspiration to the author

On the Fourth of July, 1826, Tobias "Tobey" Boland and 50 Irish laborers walked into Worcester from Uxbridge, Massachusetts. Within a short time, their ranks swelled to five hundred.

They were there to dig the Worcester section of the 46.5 mile canal that would run from Worcester to Providence, Rhode Island.

The laborers were not welcome in Worcester. They were directed to set up their shelters on the east side of town. This was the area known as "Shanty Town."

They were told to stay in Shanty Town. And they were not permitted to trespass into Worcester proper.

Tobey Boland was a very strong man. He had worked on the New York Erie Canal. Before he came to Worcester, he worked in England beginning when he was thirteen years old.

Tobey had to be strong. He came to Worcester to supervise the canal workers. They were tough men and sometimes they were difficult to control.

The canal began at Thomas Street in Worcester. By digging ditches, the workers connected a series of ponds through the Blackstone Valley until the canal flowed from Worcester to Providence, Rhode Island and out into Narragansett Bay.

The Canal sections were dug by hand. They were 32 feet wide and 3.5 feet deep. The workers were expected to remove 2.5 yards of dirt each hour and they worked 10 to 12 hours a day. They were paid nine dollars a month. Sixty locks were built to lower and lift the canal boats along the route of the canal.

The workmen labored for long hours six days each week. They dug the canal with picks and shovels and carried the dirt away in wheelbarrows.

Sunday was their day to relax and have fun. In the morning they went to church, and in the afternoon they enjoyed sporting contests. The sports included kickball, wrestling and boxing matches.

October 7, 1828 was a very special day. On that day, the first canal boat, named "Lady Carrington" arrived in Worcester. It was named in honor of Mrs. Edward Carrington, one of the early investors in the canal project.

Bands played, church bells tolled, and a number of speakers traced the history of the canal project. One of the speakers was Isaiah Thomas, who fled from British-occupied Boston during the Revolution and was the printer and editor of the first newspaper in Worcester.

It took two days for the canal boats to travel from Providence to Worcester and two days to return. From dawn to dusk, the boats were pulled by tow horses that walked along side the canal.

There were "No Swimming" signs posted by the canal. But some youngsters hopped on the canal boats for rides when the boats passed under the bridges. Some youngsters even rode the tow horses.

The canal was a busy waterway for more than 20 years. Freight and passengers were carried back and forth from Worcester to Providence.

City officials in Boston became envious of the canal since Worcester had actually become a seaport to Narragansett Bay.

The canal boats only operated between April and November. From December to March, the canal and its ponds were frozen over.

Many buildings were built along the canal. But some mill owners were upset because water from their factory ponds was diverted to the canal.

Some of the mill owners even had large rocks dropped into sections of the canal locks to prevent the boats from passing.

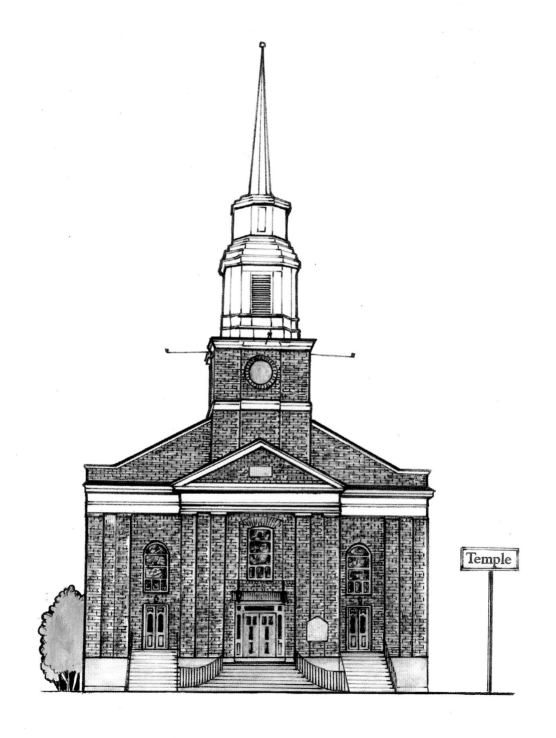

Tobey Boland was a great family man who was the father of ten children. It was Tobey who placed the cornerstone at the first Catholic church built in Worcester in 1834.

The church was called Christ Church. But when the original church building was replaced in 1846, it was renamed St. John's Church. The church was built on Temple Street.

The street and the church are still there today.

In 1835, seven years after the canal was opened, the first railroad was built between Worcester and Boston. The railroad contractor was Tobey Boland.

Construction began on the Providence and Worcester railroad in 1844. Two years later, the Massachusetts section of the canal was sold to the railroad which used the tow path as a railroad bed.

After the railroad opened there was no longer a need to ship materials on the canal. The canal was officially closed on November 9, 1848.

Tobey Boland was a man who left his mark on Worcester.

He died in Charlestown, Massachusetts in 1883.

During his life, he was a very generous man. And when he died his estate provided large funds for charities.

The City of Worcester owes a debt of gratitude
to the early canal workers.